Saint Julie Billiart

Saint Julie Billiart

The Smiling Saint

Written by

Mary Kathleen Glavich, SND

Illustrated by

James Bentley

Pauline
BOOKS & MEDIA

Boston

Library of Congress Cataloging-in-Publication Data

Glavich, Mary Kathleen.
  Saint Julie Billiart : the smiling saint / written by Mary
Kathleen Glavich ; illustrated by James Bentley.
    p. cm. — (Encounter the saints series ; 11)
  Summary: A biography of the woman who founded the
Sisters of Notre Dame de Namur, became a saint of the
Catholic Church, and lived and worked on behalf of
poor children during the difficult years of the French
Revolution.
  ISBN 0-8198-7050-1 (pbk.)
  1. Billiart, Julie, Saint, 1751–1816 — Juvenile
literature. 2. Sisters of Notre Dame de Namur Biography
— Juvenile literature. 3. Christian saints —France —
Bi-ography — Juvenile literature. [1. Billiart, Julie, Saint,
1751–1816 2. Saints. 3. Sisters of Notre Dame de
Namur. 4. Women — Biography.] I. Bentley, James,
1968 – ill. II. Title. III. Series.
  BX4700.B595 G53 2001
  271'.97 — dc21

                                    2001001847

Printed and published in the U.S.A. by Pauline Books &
Media, 50 Saint Pauls Avenue, Boston, MA 02130-3491.

www.pauline.org

Pauline Books & Media is the publishing house of the
Daughters of St. Paul, an international congregation of
women religious serving the Church with the communi-
cations media.

1 2 3 4 5 6   06 05 04 03 02 01

Encounter the Saints Series

Blesseds Jacinta and Francisco Marto
Shepherds of Fatima

Journeys with Mary
Apparitions of Our Lady

Saint Anthony of Padua
Fire and Light

Saint Bernadette Soubirous
Light in the Grotto

Saint Edith Stein
Blessed by the Cross

Saint Elizabeth Ann Seton
Daughter of America

Saint Francis of Assisi
Gentle Revolutionary

Saint Ignatius of Loyola
For the Greater Glory of God

Saint Joan of Arc
God's Soldier

Saint Julie Billiart
The Smiling Saint

Saint Maximilian Kolbe
Mary's Knight

For other children's titles on the Saints,
visit our Web site: www.pauline.org

Contents

1

Sunshine

It was July 12, 1751, and Jean François Billiart (JAH Fran SWAH BILL yahr) wasn't working in his fabric shop. Instead, under the warm sun of Cuvilly, France, he paced nervously outside his cottage, waiting. Inside one of its two rooms, his wife Marie-Louise, helped by her sister Madeleine, was giving birth to their seventh child.

Mr. Billiart thought with pain of their children who had already died. *Our first, Louise Antoinette, was only two when we lost her*, he remembered. *And a year has already gone by since both seven-year-old Marie Rose and three-year-old Bonaventure also left us.* The worried father turned to face the cottage. *If our new baby sees the light of day and is a girl, we'll name her Marie Rose Julie. Please, God, grant this child health and a long life!* Mr. Billiart prayed.

Suddenly the sound of an infant's cry broke into his thoughts. Madeleine poked her head out the door. "Congratulations, Jean!" she called excitedly. "You have a daughter! Come meet her while I get ready to take her to Saint Eloi's to be baptized. We don't want to take any chances."

Mr. Billiart's face lit up. "How can I ever thank you, Madeleine? I know you're going to be a wonderful godmother."

And so it was that from her very first day on earth, Marie Rose Julie was God's child and filled with grace. Later, when Julie, as she was familiarly called, understood the importance of baptism, she celebrated the anniversary of her baptism in a special way.

Julie grew to be a blessing to her parents. She was such a healthy, happy, and good child that neighbors commented, "God must have sent Julie to cheer her parents after the loss of their other children."

One day when Julie was three years old and playing in the yard next door, her father called her. She came running, and he scooped her up and swung her around. "Guess what, Sunshine?" he said. "God has given you a baby brother. We're naming him Louis." Holding her father's hand, Julie followed him into the house. She tiptoed to her mother's bed. Gazing at the baby in her mother's arms, she immediately loved him. Unlike Julie, Louis was a sickly and crippled child. Later Julie would help care for him as well as for Madeleine, a sister seven years older than she who was almost blind.

Julie began classes at the village school when she was seven. It was run by her uncle. Because she was bright and loved to learn, she quickly mastered reading and writing. Religion was her best subject, though. Julie memorized the questions and answers and understood her faith far better than children who were much older.

For Julie, religion wasn't just head knowledge. She loved God. Often she would sit quietly in the garden. When her mother asked, "What are you doing there so long by yourself?" Julie answered, "Talking to God." Mrs. Billiart was surprised but pleased. Louis was another matter. While Julie prayed, her mischievous little brother liked to sneak up and tickle her or throw grass at her.

"Stop bothering me, Louis!" Julie would scold. "You're such a pest! Why can't you be good?" Then, regretting her outburst, she would say, "I'm sorry, Louis. Forgive me."

In the garden Julie noticed how sunflowers turn their heads to follow the sun as it moves across the sky—even on cloudy days. Julie wanted to imitate them. Just as the sunflowers always face the sun, Julie would live always looking to God. Later she taught that to be holy is to be simple. She explained, "To be simple is to be like a sunflower, which follows all the movements of the sun and ever turns toward it." This idea became a motto that guided Julie's life: "God alone."

Fascinated by God and spiritual things as a child, Julie felt strongly drawn to share what she knew about the good God with other children.

2

PLAYING SCHOOL

"How do we know that God is good?" Eight-year-old Julie's voice caught the attention of Father Dangicourt (DAHNG ih koor) as he walked down the street. He peered into the yard and was surprised to see a young girl surrounded by a rapt crowd of children.

One girl answered, "We know God's good because he gave us all these flowers."

"And all the animals too," added a boy stroking a cat.

"God made us," a third child pointed out.

The miniature teacher with sparkling eyes lifted her arms and exclaimed, "Most of all, we know that God is good because God sent his Son Jesus to save us!"

Being new in town, Father Dangicourt inquired about the young girl and learned that she was Julie Billiart. After helping with household tasks and the family's fields, in her free time Julie loved nothing better than to teach. She taught children who couldn't

"God sent Jesus to save us!"

afford to go to school how to read and write. She gave private lessons to a beggar boy who was shunned for his crude manners. With her help, he learned not only his ABCs but also how to behave. Thirty years later he wrote Julie a letter to thank her for helping him become a successful businessman.

Julie liked to teach religion lessons best of all. She made the faith wonderful and exciting. Her warm, bubbling personality attracted the children, and her zeal for religion was contagious. Julie's young students wanted to go to her "school."

Father Dangicourt got to know Julie. He soon became her spiritual guide, helping her to grow in her faith. He taught her to pray silently in her heart and encouraged her to make sacrifices.

One day the priest stopped by to see Mr. and Mrs. Billiart. "I'm amazed at the depth of Julie's faith," he told them. "Her love for the things of God and her understanding of them are extraordinary. I see no reason why she couldn't make her First Communion now."

"You know she's only nine, Father," Mr. Billiart replied in surprise. "Children here don't receive Communion until they're thirteen or fourteen."

"Her age is no problem," assured Father Dangicourt. "Julie understands the meaning of the Eucharist. She's ready."

"But we wouldn't want to cause hard feelings by giving her this special privilege," Mrs. Billiart added in a worried tone.

"We could keep her Communions secret," the priest explained. "Julie could come to Mass early and receive Communion before anyone else arrives. I'll let her know the feast days when she may receive our Lord."

It was settled. Julie made her First Communion. Years later she wrote of it, "Never in my life have I experienced such wonder and joy as I felt that day." When she was eleven, Julie was allowed to receive Communion publicly. By then everyone knew that she was a special girl.

Every morning Julie prayed for an hour. Each day she stopped at Saint Eloi's Church to visit Jesus in the Blessed Sacrament. Before leaving, she prayed before Mary's statue. Julie read spiritual books and even thought about becoming a Carmelite sister. For her, faith was more than prayer. It was a whole way of life and was shown in action by living as Jesus did. Julie visited sick villagers and cared for them. Sometimes her parents let her stay all night with someone who was very sick or dying. People began to call Julie "the saint of Cuvilly."

At Saint Eloi's parishioners enrolled in the Confraternity of the Sacred Heart, promising to spend an hour a year praying before the Blessed Sacrament. Julie joined this association too and chose the hour from two to three on Good Friday—a time during which we especially remember Jesus' death on the cross for us. Her choice was a sign of how closely connected Julie's whole life would be to the cross of Jesus.

Another event involving the cross took place on the day of her confirmation, when she was thirteen. After the ceremony, as she was leaving the church, a Knight of Malta (a member of a respected church society) stopped Julie and gave her a relic of the true cross (a piece of the wooden cross that Jesus died on). Julie proudly inscribed on the back of the relic's container, "Given to Julie Billiart by a Knight of Malta." Then she presented the relic to her parish so that all could share it.

After her confirmation, Julie's love for God increased. One day she asked Father Dangicourt, "Father, I would like to give myself completely to God. May I please make a vow of chastity?" She intended to remain unmarried. Convinced that God was preparing Julie for a special work, Father Dangicourt agreed. At the age of fourteen Julie vowed to live for God alone.

God didn't spoil Julie as a child by giving her an easy life. She experienced the cross when her sister Marie Louise Angelique (AHN jeh LEEK) died at age twenty-one, right after she was married. Then the year after Julie's confirmation, her sixteen-year-old brother died. Julie was the only healthy child left in the family. Soon she would have new and important responsibilities.

3

THIEVES

"And what has my wife been up to while I was away?" Mr. Billiart teased as he hung his hat on the peg by the door.

"See for yourself," Mrs. Billiart grinned, planting a kiss on his cheek. "The house has been cleaned from top to bottom. Right after you left, Julie and I started spring-cleaning, and then Madeleine came over to help. We are exhausted, but you must be too."

"I am," Mr. Billiart admitted, "but it was worth it. Wait until you see the lovely lace and fine cloth I bought in town! Our store will be one of the best stocked in the world," he bragged, winking at Julie. "Maybe tomorrow you can help me arrange the goods on the shelves, Julie."

"I'd love to, Papa," she replied.

"After night prayers at Saint Eloi's I think we should all go straight to bed," Mrs. Billiart suggested.

"A good idea," agreed Mr. Billiart.

That night the family slept so soundly that no one heard thieves break into their fabric store. The next morning when Mr. Billiart went to open up, he came face to face with a nightmare. His wife and children came running at the sound of his shocked cries.

"Gone!" Mr. Billiart exclaimed. "All the bolts of new material are gone, and I haven't even paid for them yet! Look, fabric from the shelves is missing too...." He hurried to the drawer where he kept the money. "Oh, no," he groaned. "They've taken everything ...everything...."

Julie ran to the door thinking she might see the escaping thieves. "Look, Papa!" she called out. "There's some lace hanging out of the old well."

The family rushed outside and discovered that the robbers had thrown some linen and lace into the well, but all the bolts were badly damaged.

"We're ruined," moaned Mr. Billiart, burying his face in his hands.

As the weeks passed, Mr. Billiart struggled against poverty. To make matters worse, harmful reports spread about him. This caused even his friends to be suspicious of him. In order to pay his bills, Mr. Billiart sold a strip of land he had inherited. Now he had no place to grow vegetables to sell. His wife and children sadly watched him sink into depression.

One day as Julie knelt in church praying for help, she heard the Angelus bells. In those days church bells signaled everyone to stop work and pray the Angelus three times a day. Julie pictured the harvesters in the fields bowing their heads to pray. Suddenly she knew what to do. *I'll go to work in the fields,* she thought. *It's the peak of the harvest season, and the farmers are even hiring people from outside the village.*

As soon as she got home, Julie enthusiastically explained her plan to her parents. To her dismay, her father responded, "I know how you want to help, Julie, but no way is any young daughter of mine going to work with harvesters. They're too rough."

"Your father's right, Julie," her mother seconded. "The harvesters are troublemakers. They don't practice their Catholic faith. I doubt they even know what it's about."

"That's one good reason why I should go," Julie argued. "Since the harvesters don't go to church, they won't learn about God unless someone goes to teach them. Please let me do this. Don't worry that I'll be swayed by bad example. The faith I learned from you in the past sixteen years is strong."

Reluctantly Julie's parents allowed her to get a job in the fields. This turned out to be a good decision.

At first some of the other workers resented Julie. She was young and innocent. Something about her kept them from making their usual rude comments and from telling bad jokes. As time went on though, they began to accept her. They admired how hard she worked under the hot sun. This teenager could match the best of them gathering the golden wheat and binding it into sheaves. Her friendliness and her habit of singing as she worked softened their hearts. Above all, they liked her interesting stories.

During the noon break Julie would read spiritual books. One day the illiterate harvesters begged, "Read to us." As Julie read aloud, her coworkers asked her to explain what she was reading. She began telling them stories she had learned at home and from Father Dangicourt. Many of the harvesters had never heard about Moses, King David, or Jesus. They were fascinated with the stories of the Exodus, Jesus calming the storm at sea, the sower and the seed, and Jesus' resurrection. They also enjoyed singing hymns with Julie and listening to her stories that taught Christian values. Through

Julie, these field workers came to know the good God.

Little by little the group that gathered around Julie grew. Once some of the harvesters asked, "Julie, would you be able to meet with us on Sunday too?" Six workdays weren't enough to satisfy their hunger for God. "I wish I could," she replied, "but Sunday is my day for prayer and spending time with my family."

In teaching others religion, Julie was carrying out the mission God planned for her. This felt good and made her happy. Julie also had the satisfaction of knowing that her pay helped to relieve her family's financial distress a bit. Unfortunately, the harvest season ended too soon. Julie had to look for other ways to support her family.

4

TRAVELING SALESWOMAN

It was a beautiful day, but Julie could hardly wait to get home and go to bed. She had spent the night with a dying woman who had lost her faith. Near the end the woman was able to make her peace with God and die a happy death. Julie prayed, "Thank you, Lord, for the grace and love you showed her."

As Julie neared the Billiart cottage, she could hear her parents talking.

"At least you still have some customers, Jean," said her mother.

"Yes," sighed her father, "but they aren't willing to give me even half of what the merchandise is worth. How can I ever pay off my debts?"

Julie stepped inside the house. She knew her father was having little success selling the cloth the thieves had left behind. Constant worry had taken its toll on him. He looked and acted like an old man.

"Father," she asked, "isn't there anyone in Cuvilly who can pay you what is just?"

Mr. Billiart sadly shook his head. "Now in Beauvais (Boh VAY) I know I could get a better deal, but it's about twenty miles away...."

"I'll go," Julie broke in without a moment's hesitation.

"Don't be silly," replied her father. "With all the violence in our towns and on the roads these days, do you think I'd let you travel alone?"

"Jean, I know it would be risky, but it may be the only solution," Mrs. Billiart said softly.

"I'm not afraid, Papa," continued Julie. "Surely God would protect me. I could borrow a horse and be there and back in one day." She knelt down beside her father and grasped his arm. "Please let me try," she pleaded. "Please."

Mr. Billiart bent over and hugged her. "All right," he whispered. "You're such a good daughter."

The next day found Julie atop a horse with bolts of material strapped to its sides. The journey was long but not boring. Julie praised God for the birds swooping overhead, the brilliant flowers at the side of the road, and the people she passed on the way. When the horse galloped, she enjoyed the rush of the wind against her face and its whipping at her bonnet and cape. She prayed that she would find good buyers.

When she reached Beauvais, she came upon a woman walking down the road. "Could you please tell me the way to the nearest fabric shop?" Julie asked her.

The woman explained where she should go, and Julie headed her horse in that direction. At the store she dismounted and unfastened a few bolts of material. She entered the shop and walked up to a kindly-looking man at the counter.

"Excuse me, sir," she said. "I wonder if you'd be interested in purchasing some fine material."

Surprised at seeing such a young salesperson, the shopkeeper replied, "Well, let's see what you have there." He fingered some of the material and then held it up to the window. "This is very good cloth," he murmured. "Very good, indeed."

"I have more outside," said Julie cheerfully.

"Bring it in," the man directed.

To Julie's amazement and joy, the generous man bought all the fabric she had—and for full price! In no time she was on her way home again.

The taste of success was sweet. Julie began to make frequent trips to Beauvais and other neighboring towns to sell material. She traveled on foot or by horseback and sometimes even at night to sell her father's stock. When she wasn't on a business trip, she embroidered church vestments and made lace, supplying the Carmelite sisters. One wealthy woman put Julie in charge of distributing her charitable gifts. For six years during harvest time, Julie also worked in the fields. Despite these many activities, she always made time for daily Mass.

One day Julie noticed that everything looked blurred to her. She nervously hoped and prayed that her vision would improve, but as the days passed, it only got worse. Finally she told her parents about it.

"Oh, no! Not both you and Madeleine!" her mother wailed. "My poor children!"

Julie was taken to a doctor. He predicted that she would eventually go completely blind. Undaunted, Mrs. Billiart turned to God. She planned a family pilgrimage to a monastery of the Cistercian monks in Montreuil (Mon TROOL). There a replica of the Holy Face was honored. This was an image of Jesus left on Veronica's veil after she used it to wipe his face on the way to Calvary. At

Montreuil God favored the Billiarts with a double miracle—both Madeleine and Julie received their sight back!

Her vision restored, Julie returned to her normal work and acts of charity. Soon, however, she would have a much heavier cross to carry.

5

A Smiling Sufferer

Julie's life changed drastically in 1774 when she was twenty-three. One winter evening she and her father were sitting alone in the fabric shop talking. Suddenly there was a loud crash as a window shattered. A rock rolled across the floor to their feet. "Papa!" Julie screamed, jumping up. With that, a shot rang out, and a bullet whizzed by, just missing Mr. Billiart's head. The sound of running feet echoed down the street.

Stunned, Julie stared in horror at her father. "Papa, you could have been killed!" she exclaimed. He pressed his arms around her. She was trembling violently. "There, there," he soothed, rocking her back and forth and smoothing her hair.

"Why would…anyone…try to hurt you?" Julie stammered.

"Who knows?" said Mr. Billiart. "Today people are beaten and attacked for no reason at all. We're both all right, though. Thank God."

"Papa, you could have been killed!"

But Julie was not all right. And she wouldn't be for a long time. The shock of that night made her very sick. She had experienced neuralgia, a painful nerve condition, before, but now it returned, worse than ever. Pain gripped her body and her muscles became weaker.

Julie kept up her work as much as she could. She continued her needlework. She prepared children for First Communion. Using crutches she walked to church and to the homes of the sick. She told them, "God understands. He suffered once too. Never forget: God loves you more than anyone else in the world." Julie brought everyone the kindness and care of Jesus. She brought them laughter and hope. People wondered, *How can one who suffers so much smile so much?*

Julie's reputation for goodness and courage spread. The bishop of Beauveau asked to meet this "saint of Cuvilly." Julie and her father visited him, and the bishop had a chance to see her wisdom and holiness firsthand. After Julie left, he commented, "That young girl seems to be inspired by God himself. I will be surprised if we do not hear more of her later."

Eight years after the attack on the Billiarts' shop, a terrible fever broke out in Cuvilly. It soon reached epidemic proportions. Doctors at that time thought that illness was in the blood. They treated patients by bleeding them, a process in which they drained certain amounts of blood from the sick. The local doctor thought this treatment would help Julie. For sixth months he regularly bled her. This only made her condition worse. Her legs became paralyzed so that she couldn't stand or take a step. She could hardly eat. Sometimes her body shook uncontrollably. Five times Julie was at the point of death, and Father Dangicourt came to anoint her. She bore her suffering patiently. As long as she could, she embroidered articles for the church and continued to make and sell lace to support herself.

Now that Julie couldn't go out, people came to her. A door was made from her room to the street outside. Through it passed Father Dangicourt with daily Holy Communion, children coming to learn their catechism lessons, and grownups who came to ask for prayers and guidance. Fine ladies from Paris who had summerhouses in Cuvilly also visited. Madeleine's seven-year-old daughter, Felicité (Feh LISS ih tay), began helping to take care of her Aunt Julie. One of Felicité's tasks was to invite children to religion lessons.

All these visitors loved Julie. She showed them how to love God. They called her "the saint." One wealthy count admired Julie so much that in his will he left her six hundred francs each year.

Julie's paralysis eventually spread to the muscles of her jaw. Because of this she was often unable to speak. In this helpless state she could no longer be a support to her family. In fact, she was a burden. Her total dependence on others must have been a terrible hardship for Julie. She had always been so independent. Unable to do much else, Julie spent many hours of her long days and nights praying. People often saw her in deep, peaceful contemplation, totally wrapped up in God. In these hours she was unaware of what was around her, until someone would gently shake her. Through illness and prayer, God was shaping her for a future mission.

6

THE REVOLUTION

While Julie was in bed, paralyzed, France was in turmoil. Common people were discontent with the government and the Church. Taxes were high, and a crop failure led to a food shortage and exorbitant prices. People complained, "While we starve, our rulers, the nobility, and some clergy and religious live in luxury." The freedom and equality that new philosophers were teaching sounded good. For the unhappy people, the French Revolution was the answer.

In 1789 the Bastille, a prison, was stormed, freeing many prisoners whose only crime was not having paid their debts. A new government, which viewed the Church as an enemy, was set up. The slaughter of the ruling class and the attack on the Church began. Priests were required to sign an oath supporting the new government instead of the Pope. Those who didn't take this oath and join the schismatic (breakaway) church were persecuted. In the name of freedom, revolutionaries rioted and killed like maniacs. Many innocent people were beheaded at the guillotine (a machine with a sharp blade that was used to cut off a person's head). This era is well named the Reign of Terror.

Confused and frightened people found comfort and advice in Julie's room. "God is good," she assured them. "God is good."

One of Julie's faithful visitors was Father Dangicourt. "Julie," he said one day, standing at the side of her bed, "you know I can never take the oath."

"Of course not," she agreed. "It makes me sad to see so many priests leaving the true Church. May God give you the courage to be firm."

"With the help of some parishioners, I'll be going into hiding," Father Dangicourt confided. "There's a small hut behind a chicken coop. It will be my home for awhile."

"I suppose I won't see you then," Julie said with deep regret. "At least I have the cat you gave me to remind me of you." She glanced down at the large purring cat curled up beside her feet.

"Don't worry," Father Dangicourt replied. "I'll still come to your room and celebrate Mass for you and your friends some nights."

"But, Father," Julie protested, "that will be so dangerous!"

"We'll just have to trust God, won't we?" the priest answered with a little smile.

Six months later Father Dangicourt fled to a monastery for protection. He died a few months afterward.

A new priest, one who had taken the government-imposed oath and had left the Church, was assigned to Cuvilly. Julie refused to let him visit her. She told people, "Better to have no Mass at all than one celebrated by a schismatic priest." In the meantime she helped arrange hiding places for the faithful priests.

This paralyzed woman was a serious threat to the revolutionaries!

7

ESCAPE!

One day, Madame de Pont l'Abbé (POHNT lah BAY), a friend of Julie's, told her, "Your life is in danger. You must leave Cuvilly. Come to my chateau. You can hide there."

"Aunt Julie, may I go with you?" Felicité begged. "I'm sixteen now. I'm sure my parents would let me."

Felicité's parents gave their permission, and Julie agreed to go. It would be safer to stay at the chateau, a large mansion located out in the country, than it would be to remain in the village.

Arrangements were made, and Madame de Pont returned in her carriage for Julie and Felicité. Julie didn't know when or if she would ever see her parents again. Shortly after, Madame de Pont had to flee for her life to England, where she died.

The new owners of the chateau tried to keep Julie's presence a secret, but a group of revolutionaries discovered she was there. One night they tore down an outdoor shrine

"We must hurry…"

of Calvary and made a bonfire. They added the tabernacle, statues, and religious books from the parish church to the fire. Now it was big enough to burn Julie alive—which was exactly what they intended to do!

The mob raced toward the chateau.

"We must hurry!" the caretaker cried to Julie. "They're coming for you! You can hide in the hay cart." He carried Julie outside. Felicité followed. The good man laid Julie on the floor of the wagon, and Felicité climbed in. Quickly he covered both of them with hay.

The courageous caretaker ran back to the chateau. He met the mob at the door. The revolutionaries swarmed past him into the house. "Where is she?" one screeched. "Give us the saint!"

"She's not here," the caretaker replied.

"Come on! We know she's here," a drunken man shouted. "We'll find her!" Turning to the others he cried, "Let's go!"

The raving men ran through the house. "We'll drag the invalid from her bed and toss her in a blanket," one yelled. "We'll watch her dance!"

Not finding Julie, the mob finally left. "We'll be back!" they threatened. On his way out one revolutionary carved a message on the wall: "Stuff the aristocrats with bullets."

The caretaker and a younger man who lived at the chateau ran to the hay cart. "We have to leave before they return," the caretaker panted. The two men hurriedly hitched a horse to the wagon and drove down the road—straight through the wild mob! Julie, struggling to breathe under the hay, could hear the cursing and threats of the crowd. The rough ride caused her paralyzed body severe pain. But the blasphemy of the revolutionaries hurt Julie even more.

In the early hours of the morning when it was still dark, the travelers arrived in Compiègne (Com PIEN), a town twenty miles away. They stopped at the courtyard of an inn. The men lifted Julie off the cart and set her on a bench.

"You're not just going to leave us here, are you?" Felicité asked in a shaky voice. "It's freezing!"

"I'm sorry," said the caretaker. "We've done all we could." And the two men, who would face punishment if caught, drove off.

Very worried about Julie, Felicité tried to get her to drink some wine and kept rubbing her hands to warm her. Finally two women who were sisters came upon Julie and Felicité shivering from the cold. "You can live with us," they invited.

For two months Julie and Felicité stayed as guests of the two sisters. Then one of them broke the bad news. "We're sorry," she apologized, "but we have to ask you to leave our house. It's just too dangerous to keep you here. You're still being hunted by the revolutionaries."

During the next three and a half years, Julie had to move five times. Her favorite short prayer then was, "Lord, will you not lodge me in your paradise, since I can no longer find a shelter on earth?"

In 1793 Father de LaMarche, a priest in hiding who ministered to faithful people in Compiègne, began to care for Julie's spiritual needs too. Amazingly, whenever he came, she regained her power of speech (her paralysis still often prevented her from speaking) and was able to receive the sacrament of Reconciliation. The priest marveled at Julie's unwavering faith in the good God, which gave her the strength to endure her sufferings.

Julie lived not only in fear for herself, but also for her family. Her health worsened to the point that she almost entirely lost her power of speech. A fresh cross was hearing of her father's death in 1792 and not being with her family to comfort them.

As Julie lived from day to day, making lace for a living, she occasionally heard reports of the horrible things happening in her country. She learned of the execution of some of her friends, including the Carmelite nuns. When the sixteen Carmelites approached the guillotine, Father de LaMarche was with them in disguise and managed to bless them. Bravely they sang the "Salve Regina," a hymn to Mary, until there was only one sister left. Then her voice too was silenced.

At this time Julie had a vision which also gave her hope. On Good Friday she saw Jesus on the cross. Around the cross were standing a group of sisters wearing an unfamiliar habit, or religious clothing. She saw some faces so clearly that later she could recognize them when she met them in person. Then she heard a voice saying, "Behold the daughters whom I give to you in the institute which will be marked by my cross." After this, God also let Julie see in her imagination some of the trials she would undergo in the future.

Soon things happened that paved the way for the fulfillment of her vision and its prophecy. Julie's friend Madame Baudoin (Bow DWAH) had lost her father and her husband to the guillotine. She was moving to Amiens (AH mee EN) with her three daughters. She invited Julie to join them, begging Julie to come and support her in her time of need. She had arranged for Julie to have rooms in the Hôtel Blin (BLIH), the house of Count Blin de Bourdon. At first Julie's response was no. Unable to speak, she wrote on paper to Felicité, "The ride to Amiens is impossible for me in my condition."

After receiving two more letters from Madame Baudoin, Julie felt she couldn't refuse her friend's request. Although the trip would be long and painful, Julie agreed to go to Amiens. On the way there she stopped in Cuvilly and saw her mother for the last time.

God had a plan for Julie. And this journey would lead her to the person destined to help make her dreams come true.

8

FRANÇOISE

It was October of 1794 when Julie and Felicité arrived in Amiens. Felicité carried Julie up the stairs to their quarters in the Hôtel Blin. At that home Julie would meet Françoise (Fran SWAHZ) Blin de Bourdon, Count Blin de Bourdon's sister. Françoise would become her life-long friend and helper. Françoise was the person Julie had seen most clearly in her vision of the cross.

Françoise's background was quite different from Julie's. She was born in 1756 and raised in her grandmother's home, Gezaincourt (GEH zayn kour). As a member of the nobility, Françoise was presented at the court of King Louis XVI when she was eighteen. Then she went to care for her grandmother. In February 1794, when Françoise was thirty-eight years old, revolutionaries came to arrest her grandmother. The household servants, armed only with pitchforks and shovels, went out to meet them.

"Go home," Françoise ordered the servants. "I'll deal with these people. Don't worry. All will work out." The servants obediently left.

Turning to the mob, Françoise then bargained, "I'll go with you if you leave my grandmother in peace."

Satisfied, the revolutionaries arrested Françoise and took her to prison in a cart. She learned that her father, brother, and nephew were also prisoners. The following month her grandmother died. The older woman had refused to eat until Françoise returned.

In prison one day Françoise happened to see a newspaper. She and her whole family were on the list to be guillotined during the next weeks! Fortunately, changes in the government occurred before their execution was carried out. In August 1794, Françoise was allowed to return to her brother's home. She arrived a few months before Julie came to the Hôtel Blin.

Before long, Françoise, Madame Baudoin's seventeen-year-old daughter Lise, and four of Lise's friends became regular visitors to Julie's room. They were attracted by her deep spirituality. Although Françoise later admitted that Julie's trouble in speaking had at first repelled her, she came to Julie's room often to bring her soup or to read to her. Françoise confided to Julie that her dream was to be a Carmelite nun someday.

The six women grew to love the invalid. Lise's friends moved into the Hôtel Blin. A community was formed around Julie, whom the women called "Mother" or "Mother Julie." A priest named Father Thomas became their chaplain. A professor in Paris before the revolution, Father Thomas had been imprisoned and condemned to the guillotine for not taking the oath to support the government rather than the Pope. He was free now, but still in danger.

Another cross came to Julie when Françoise was called away to care for her dying father. By this time she and Julie were close friends. Julie wrote to her, "My good and loving friend, my heart will never be able to express how dear you are to me." In the future Françoise would devote her entire fortune to carrying out Mother Julie's work. Although they came from different classes of society, these two women became so united that Julie once remarked that they were like "two heads under one bonnet."

9

FLIGHT AGAIN

In 1797 a new religious persecution broke out in France. The government required priests to take another oath. Again Father Thomas refused. Three times guards trooped through the Hôtel Blin searching for him. The third time he ran to the stable. A drunken guard raced after him. The priest climbed the ladder to the hayloft. But before he could pull the ladder up and out of reach, the guard was there, setting down a candle in the darkness.

"I've caught our bird!" the intoxicated guard yelled to his companions.

With that, the candle fell over, and the flame sputtered out. As the guard bent to retrieve it, Father Thomas leaped over his head to freedom.

Back at the Hôtel Blin the little community of women was overjoyed to hear that their chaplain had escaped. Josephine, a member of the group, then spoke up. "We can't stay here any longer. It isn't safe."

Everyone agreed.

"But where can we go?" Julie asked.

"I have a small estate outside the city, in Bettencourt, twenty miles away," Josephine offered. "We can hide there."

That very night Father Thomas, Julie, Françoise, Josephine, and Felicité fled in a carriage to Bettencourt. Soon after they arrived, Julie became seriously ill, and Françoise came down with smallpox. They both recovered. In fact, Julie experienced better health than she had for years. With Father Thomas coaching her every day, her speech returned. She was also well enough to sit in a chair. The little community was ready to begin its work of restoring the Catholic faith in France.

Not until 1799 were French Catholics free to practice their faith again. For seven years schools and churches had been closed. Many people had lost or forgotten their faith. Children had not been taught it. Father Thomas began to instruct the men and boys of Bettencourt, while Julie and Françoise taught the women and girls.

In 1803, after four years in Bettencourt, Father Thomas told Julie and Françoise, "It's time we return to Amiens. The need to teach the faith is even greater there."

On the day the religion teachers left, the villagers cried.

While in Bettencourt, Felicité had fallen in love with a teacher in a nearby village. After seeing that Julie was settled in Amiens, she left her in the care of Françoise and another woman. Felicité had served her aunt well for twenty-two years.

10

A NEW COMMUNITY

Father Varin was the head of the Fathers of the Faith, as the Society of Jesus or the Jesuits were then called. He had seen Julie's work in Bettencourt and was impressed. He and Father Thomas encouraged Julie to begin a community of religious sisters dedicated to the education of children. "Imagine how many more poor children you would reach if you had a group of women to help you," Father Varin kept insisting.

By this time, though, all the young women who had lived with Julie at the Hôtel Blin had left to follow other paths in life. Only Françoise remained. Julie wondered how the vision she had seen of a new community of sisters would ever be fulfilled. She was also thinking, *How can I start a religious community when I can hardly take care of myself?*

In Amiens Julie continued to gather children for religion lessons. Finally Father Varin and the presence of many orphans in the streets persuaded her to pray for other women to come and help her. Julie and Françoise moved into a large, vacant orphanage on the Rue Nueve. Father Varin sent them eight poor orphan girls to care for.

One day a young woman named Catherine Duchatel came to visit. "I was with the Ladies of the Sacred Heart, who educate the daughters of the wealthy," she explained to Julie. "But my heart is really drawn to poor children. May I join you and Françoise in your work?"

"Of course!" Julie beamed, and she welcomed Catherine with joy.

On February 2, 1804, Father Varin celebrated a special Mass in the chapel of the orphanage. During this Mass, Julie, Françoise, and Catherine consecrated themselves to God as sisters and promised to devote their lives to the education of orphans and the formation of teachers. The new community was to be called the Sisters of Notre Dame. *Notre Dame* (NOHTR DAHM) is French for "Our Lady." The sisters were to try to imitate the spirit and virtue, strength and compassion of Mary. She would be their patroness. Julie was to be the first Mother or leader of the community.

This was the small, humble beginning of the Sisters of Notre Dame. Years later Cardinal Sterckx said, "What is the Institute of Notre Dame? A breath of the apostolic spirit fallen on the heart of a woman who knew how to believe and how to love."

Later that month two other women asked to enter the new community. They were soon joined by a third. In addition to teaching the orphans, the sisters began catechism classes. In her lively lessons, Mother Julie often sang hymns. One person remarked, "When Mother Julie sings, it's love singing love."

That year was a jubilee year, a special time to celebrate the restoration of the faith in Rome. Missions (religious renewals) were carried out in all the churches. For years people had been deprived of hearing about the Catholic faith. Now they thronged the churches. Five or six times a week Mother Julie was carried in a chair to the cathedral to instruct women and girls in religion. Through Mother Julie and her companions they came to have hope in God and his Church again.

One of the missionaries was a young, zealous priest named Father Enfantin (AH fah tih). During the mission he stayed at the sisters' convent. Father Varin appointed him to be Mother Julie's spiritual guide, even though at fifty-three, Julie was almost twice Father Enfantin's age.

Because of Father Enfantin, Mother Julie's life would be changed in a way she never expected…

11

THE MIRACLE

On May 28, 1804, the last day of the mission, Mother Julie and Father Enfantin were in the parlor talking. The priest stood to leave. Turning to Mother Julie he said, "By the way, would you please join me in a novena of prayer to the Sacred Heart for someone in whom I'm interested?"

"Of course," Mother Julie replied. "I've had a special devotion to the Sacred Heart of Jesus since I was a child. I'll be glad to pray for your friend."

June is the month the Church dedicates to the Sacred Heart. Father Enfantin gave a powerful sermon on June 1, which was the First Friday, a day people especially honor the Sacred Heart of Jesus by receiving Holy Communion. After Mass Father strode into the garden where Mother Julie was seated in her chair. Looking directly at her, he challenged, "Mother, if you have any faith, take one step in honor of the Sacred Heart of Jesus!"

Mother Julie stood, and for the first time in twenty-two years, took a step. The friend she had prayed for had been herself!

"Take another," the priest ordered. Mother Julie took another step. "Another," he urged. And Julie took a third step. "That will do," Father Enfantin said with a smile. "You may sit down now."

"I could still walk more," Mother Julie declared.

"No, that's enough," Father replied. "Now don't tell the sisters about this until the novena is finished."

"All right," Mother Julie agreed, tears glistening in her eyes. Julie returned to her chair, and Father Enfantin left. *How good God is to me,* she thought. *May my steps always be for his greater glory.*

Unable to keep her joy to herself, Julie confided to Father Thomas that she could walk. She proved it by quickly climbing the stairs. Father Thomas wept for joy. But Mother Julie kept her promise and didn't let the sisters know that she was healed. She continued to remain in her chair, and she climbed the stairs by sitting and using her hands to push herself up each step.

June 5 marked the end of the novena. That morning after Mass everyone went downstairs for breakfast—everyone except Julie. While the others were eating, she quietly came down the stairway. One little girl, seeing her, cried out, "Mother is walking downstairs!" The sisters and children knelt in awe and thanked God for the miracle.

"Come to chapel with me," Mother Julie invited. "Let's sing the 'Te Deum' to thank God for this marvelous gift." The group went to chapel where they sang with all their hearts.

Word spread among the villagers that Julie could walk again. "God must have great work in store for her," they concluded.

Father Enfantin didn't want Mother Julie to become proud about what God had done for her. In fact, he took extreme measures to prevent this. After her cure, he had her make a ten-day silent retreat. This was the beginning of a whole year in which he tried to strengthen Julie's virtue through acts of self-denial, discipline, and humility. But outside of her earshot, he told people, "I have never met such a holy and remarkable woman!"

At the end of the retreat, Mother Julie and another sister went to help with a mission in a nearby town. One day as the two walked to religion class, a carriage almost ran them over. As Julie jumped out of the way, she sprained her ankle. Later Father Varin saw her limping. *She's not really cured,* he thought, not knowing of the accident. Mother Julie went into church to pray. When she came out, her foot was normal again.

In July Father Varin presented the young community of sisters with a rule of life approved by Bishop Demandolx (DEH mah dole) of Amiens. In October the sisters pronounced their religious vows according to this rule. The next day the sisters elected Julie as their Mother General, or leader.

Shortly after, both Father Thomas and Father Varin left for other work. Father Varin put the small community of sisters in the hands of Father LeBlanc (Luh BLAH), superior of the Fathers of the Faith in Amiens. He also appointed a young priest named Father de Sambucy (Sam BOO see) as the sisters' confessor.

This last decision was a great mistake.

12

TEACHING

"I hope Mother Julie will teach us to-day," little Anne said to Marie as the two orphans finished breakfast.

"Me, too," Marie responded. "Maybe she'll have surprises in her pockets again."

"I like the surprises, but even more I like the way Mother Julie talks to us," continued Anne. "When she talks about God, I want to be good every day. I know I won't always be, but at least I want to try."

Mother Julie's days were filled with business: meeting with bishops, landlords, and officials and making plans. Yet Julie taught religion to the children whenever she could. She never sat when she taught but walked around. She sang a lot and let the children put on plays. Best of all, she made them realize how much God cared for them. Her goodness touched the children's hearts. Most of Mother Julie's time, however, was spent instructing their teachers.

Julie prepared her sisters to teach. She told them, "You must not just talk about love to the children, you must *show* them how God loves them," and "Catechists must see God in the children and believe in the greatness of their work." To train the sisters, practical Julie would sometimes say, "Look, suppose I'm an old woman who comes to you for instructions. I have not practiced the faith for forty years. Now begin to teach me."

Mother Julie also trained the sisters in religious life. She taught them, "We have been captivated by the divine charm of our good Jesus. His love has amazed us, and we have been made his captives." Aware of the importance of prayer, Julie instructed her sisters, "If you do not become souls of prayer, our Institute will perish." Mother Julie reminded one novice who didn't expect religious life to be so hard, "You don't get to heaven on wheels, Sister. You walk!"

The life of the first Sisters of Notre Dame was difficult. The children they cared for were usually undernourished, dirty, and sick. Because of unclean conditions, the children were often infected with tiny insects called lice. Despite the challenging job of teaching these poor children, the sisters spent much time in prayer. Every day they went to Mass, prayed an hour in the morning and a half-hour in the evening, and prayed the rosary.

The sisters were poor. They ate bread and water in the morning and soup and vegetables for dinner. Meat was eaten only on Sundays and feast days. The sisters slept on straw mattresses on the floor of a large dormitory. Their clothes were dyed violet and didn't always fit right. More than one woman probably commented, "Look at Françoise in that short skirt…. It's disgraceful how that noblewoman goes about in public now. She must have lost her mind!"

But even with all the problems they faced, the sisters were happy. Their numbers continued to grow. So did the number of their students. One day Mother Julie had a hint of more growth than she ever imagined.

It was February 2, 1806, the feast of the Presentation of Jesus in the Temple. Mother Julie was giving the sisters a talk about the feast. At one point, she broke into song, praying the "Nunc Dimittis," the canticle of Simeon, the elderly man who recognized the infant Jesus in the Temple. When she came to the words "a light of revelation to the gentiles," she stopped and looked at the crucifix. Julie became perfectly still, staring at the crucifix. Light shone from her face, and she was raised above the floor. She remained like this until some noises brought her back to her senses. Then she immediately left the room.

Later, Mother Julie explained to Françoise what had happened: "God let me know that we will carry the light of the Gospel to all nations. We are not to be limited to one diocese or country." This vision was in line with Julie's teaching. She urged her sisters to have a heart as wide as the world. Her religious order would require missionary souls who were willing to go wherever they were needed.

Not long after, Mother Julie visited the bishop of Ghent, in Flanders, a region of Belgium. Before she left, he told her, "I would like sisters in Flanders."

"Your Excellency," Mother Julie replied, "my sisters don't speak Flemish, only French. We would need women who speak Flemish to join us."

"I'll find some," the bishop promised.

When Mother Julie returned to Amiens, France, she brought with her the first woman from Flanders. The woman didn't speak any French, yet, after meeting Mother Julie, she was willing to go with her to France.

The community of sisters moved into a larger house when it reached eighteen members. Mother Julie then had space to hold free classes for poor children. One day she sent for a novice and postulant, young women who were being formed as sisters. She gave them each a bell. "Walk through the streets and ring these bells," she instructed. "Tell people about our school." The young women did, proclaiming, "The Sisters of Notre Dame have just opened free schools for little girls!"

Boys and girls in tattered clothes heard the music of the bells. They stopped playing tag, kicking stones, and making mudpies. They followed the sound. Crowding around one bell ringer, they looked up at her with big eyes and dirty faces. "Who are you?" they asked.

"I'm a sister," she explained. "You girls are invited to come to our school for free. Go tell your parents."

The bells were a success. On the first day of school, sixty children showed up.

Then the bishop of Ghent asked Julie to teach in a school at Saint Nicolas in his diocese. Three sisters, including a Flemish one, began the second Notre Dame convent. Mother Julie stayed with them for two months to help them get started. In Flanders the sisters were able to wear the religious habit, which Julie designed based on her vision at Compiègne. (The government did not allow them to wear the habit in France.) During Mother Julie's stay in Flanders the bishop also asked her to take over another school.

Next, Bishop Pisani of Namur (Na MOOR), Belgium, invited Julie to open a school in his diocese. She went to visit him. When she returned to Amiens, the sisters had more exciting news to share. "A priest from Mondidier (Mon DIH Dee AY) came while you were away, Mother. He also wants us to open a school in his town."

The work of the sisters was being blessed by God. Soon God would also bless it with the cross.

13

TROUBLE

Although Father de Sambucy was only the sisters' confessor, he saw himself as their founder. He wanted to make the decisions and to guide the sisters. When Mother Julie gave young sisters advice about the spiritual life, he objected. *She's only a woman,* he thought. *She doesn't have the education to give spiritual guidance, and she's from the poor class of society besides.*

Father de Sambucy and Mother Julie did not agree on several matters. He didn't like having convents outside of Amiens, and he resented Mother Julie's frequent trips. Neither did he approve when Mother Julie sometimes allowed exceptions to the rule. This young priest began taking steps to get rid of Mother Julie.

One thing he did was to write letters to Bishop Demandolx, accusing Julie of being a proud, ambitious woman who lacked the skills to govern a religious community. He sent similar letters to her friends in other communities. Another strategy he used was to get the bishop to change his mind about the sister who had been appointed superior of the new convent in Namur. Sister Françoise was sent instead. With Françoise gone from Amiens, Father de Sambucy could freely work against Mother Julie.

As Julie and the small group of sisters were leaving Amiens for Namur, Father de Sambucy turned to Mother Julie. "You've finished your business here," he said. "You may now go and do it elsewhere."

Finally, and what was probably most painful to Mother Julie, Father de Sambucy intercepted letters between Mother Julie and Françoise, and their Amiens community.

The day after Mother Julie left town, the bishop put Father de Sambucy in charge of the sisters in place of Father LeBlanc.

Father de Sambucy assembled the sisters in Amiens and announced that he was going to reorganize them. "Sister Thérèse will be your superior from now on," he declared. "I'm changing her name to Mother Victoire (Vic TWAHR). She will report to me about everything in the community."

Sister Thérèse was only twenty-three years old. She wasn't prepared to lead the

"You've finished your business here."

community. Her name change was a sign of Father de Sambucy's victory.

One day, after opening a new convent in Bordeaux, Mother Julie received a letter from Bishop Demandolx. The letter requested her to return to Amiens. On the way there, Julie stopped at the convents of two different religious communities where the superiors were her friends. But both of these sisters seemed less friendly than usual. Julie couldn't understand what had happened. The second superior handed her a letter from Bishop Demandolx. In it he contradicted his first order. He forbade Mother Julie to return to her convent in Amiens or even to set foot in his diocese! Devastated, Mother Julie found her way to the convent chapel. For two hours she prayed before the tabernacle. From Jesus she received the courage to accept God's will.

Seeking guidance and support, Mother Julie then went to see Father Varin, who had always helped her. But Father de Sambucy had reached him first, accusing Julie of all kinds of things. Because of this, Father Varin also rejected Julie.

Mother Julie wrote to Bishop Demandolx asking forgiveness for whatever she had done to displease him. She even went to visit him, although she was sick. "Go back to Namur," the bishop ordered. Then realizing that she was very ill, he gave in. "All right," he said. "You may return to your convent in Amiens until you recover."

At Amiens, Mother Julie crept secretly up the back stairs to her room. Word spread that she was there, and the sisters came to see her. They told her that Mother Victoire had not been a capable superior and that Bishop Demandolx was threatening to put an Ursuline sister in charge of the convent.

Eventually the bishop made Mother Julie superior again. But neither Mother Victoire nor Father de Sambucy accepted the change. Both continued to exert control over the community.

During this time Mother Julie was asked to start a new convent in Jumet, Belgium. Bishop Demandolx would not allow her to go with the sisters to found the house. He also refused to send Mother Victoire there as Julie had planned. As a result, the young sisters who went to open the house were left rather helpless in the face of major difficulties. In the end the bishop had to send Mother Julie to Jumet to straighten out matters.

With typical faith, Mother Julie explained all her trials in a letter to Françoise, "The good God must have some hidden design in all this, for everything to be so disturbed without reason." All her life Mother Julie calmly faced frustrations and sufferings, trusting that somehow God would draw good from them.

Things only got worse when Father de Sambucy and another priest wrote a new rule for the sisters. Mother Julie and Sister Françoise could not accept it because it limited them to staying in Amiens. Mother Julie went to consult her friend Father Varin about the matter. When she arrived, she delivered a letter to him from Father de Sambucy, unaware that it condemned her. After reading this letter, Father Varin exploded in anger. "Father de Sambucy is to write your rule!" he shouted. "You are to return to Amiens and stay there." Shocked at this outburst, Mother Julie became ill. She returned to Amiens and waited for the Lord to act.

Once again Bishop Demandolx sent for her. He raged in anger about the way Mother Victoire was being treated, even stamping his foot for emphasis. Julie left his house in tears. She didn't know then that his strange behavior was probably due to a brain tumor the bishop was suffering from.

One day when Mother Julie returned to Amiens after visiting the other sisters, she was greeted with more bad news. A typhoid epidemic had put twenty-three sisters in bed. Mother Julie went to the infirmary and called, "My children, if you have faith, rise." All but four sisters got up, feeling better.

In the end, the crisis in Amiens was resolved when God directly showed Mother Julie the way. Bishop Demandolx sent Julie a letter that gave her relief but made her sad. In it he wrote that because she was guiding the sisters differently from what he expected, she was free to leave and go to any other diocese. He would form "true Sisters of Notre Dame in Amiens." The sisters then in Amiens were to choose to remain there or to go with Mother Julie to Namur, Belgium.

Julie presented this choice to the sisters. "I will accept anyone who wishes to come," she explained. "And I will feel no ill will toward anyone who prefers to remain."

All the sisters answered, "We'll go with you!"

But later, Father de Sambucy persuaded Mother Victoire to stay behind.

14

TO NAMUR

On a cold, snowy January 15 in 1809 Mother Julie and five sisters said a tearful goodbye to Amiens and set out for Namur. Sister Françoise and the other sisters were to follow later. Julie instructed Françoise to write to Bishop Pisani of Namur. "Tell him that we can now accept the invitation he gave me a few years ago to open a school in Namur, and that we're on our way," Julie told Françoise. "Explain that Bishop Demandolx has given us the freedom to leave his diocese, since he wants to guide the sisters differently and he doesn't wish us to work outside of Amiens."

How painful it must have been for Julie to leave not only her country, but the house and city where her congregation had begun. To make matters worse, when the carriage driver arrived and saw how much baggage the sisters had with them, he wasn't happy.

"I can't take all this on one trip," he argued. "It's too heavy!"

"If the baggage doesn't go, I don't either," Mother Julie calmly responded. "In that case we don't have any need of you or your carriage." She then went to the garden to give the driver time to think. When she returned, he sullenly gave in. "All right," he said. "I'll take all of you, but it won't be easy."

At one point on the journey the horses started slipping on the icy roads. The driver made the sisters get out and walk for more than fifteen miles in the snow and ice!

One evening the carriage stopped at a rundown inn in a deserted field. As the sisters entered, a group of men looked them over. "We'll be back," they told the innkeeper.

When Mother Julie stepped outside again, a young man approached her. "This is no place for you," he quietly warned. "Try to go further on. Don't stay here." Then he disappeared. Another sister had the same message conveyed to her by a woman. This messenger also strangely disappeared.

Scarcely knowing how it happened, Mother Julie convinced the driver to leave. In no time the sisters were back in the carriage. The innkeeper's angry shouts followed them as they drove away. In telling the story later, Mother Julie said, "God, by means of his angels, delivered us from a great danger."

In Namur, Mother Julie went directly to Bishop Pisani. Unfortunately, letters from Bishop Demandolx and Father de Sambucy had arrived ahead of her and had set the bishop's mind against her. On top of everything else, Bishop Pisani hadn't read the letter that Sister Françoise had sent. The bishop greeted Julie coldly, "You come to Namur uninvited, Sister, taking it on yourself to uproot a community in the dead of winter?"

"Didn't you receive Sister Françoise's letter, Your Excellency?" Mother Julie asked in surprise. "It explained why we were coming."

When Bishop Pisani found and read the letter, he made Julie more welcome. But her reputation had been damaged, and it was repeatedly attacked in other letters that Father de Sambucy sent the bishop. Julie had to win Bishop Pisani's trust. After interviewing each sister, the bishop finally realized that Mother Julie was not the tyrant she was painted to be in Father de Sambucy's letters.

In the meantime, Françoise and the other sisters still in Amiens were also under attack. Priests threatened and pressured them to separate from Julie and stay in Amiens.

One tall visiting priest shouted at Françoise, "How can you even think of following that woman? She's full of illusions!" He went on ranting and raving for several minutes. Finally Sister Françoise stood. "Please pray for me," she said quietly.

A little more subdued, the priest promised, "I'll keep you in my prayers," and left.

The sisters at Amiens remained strong in their loyalty to Mother Julie. Soon all but Mother Victoire left Amiens to join Julie and the others in Namur, Belgium.

But some of the Sisters of Notre Dame living in the smaller French convents were persuaded to leave Mother Julie's congregation. They moved into the empty Amiens convent with Mother Victoire. Father de Sambucy also convinced a few sisters from a different religious order to join them. This new group lived under Bishop Demandolx's direction. He considered them Sisters of Notre Dame, even though they now had nothing to do with Mother Julie.

Throughout all her trials, Julie practiced what she advised her sisters: courage and confidence. At one point she admitted that her burden was "heavy enough to kill ten poor Julies like me." Yet, she never stopped repeating her motto, "How good is the good God!" or as she used to say in French, "Qu'il il est bon, le bon Dieu!"

15

ENERGY

During the next few years, Mother Julie showed unusual energy for someone her age. She lived out the sayings she is known for: "Plenty of energy but no fuss," and "Better mistakes than paralysis." A sister once remarked, "Mother Julie was everywhere at once, and somehow you always felt better for having seen her."

To make it possible for all the sisters to make a weeklong retreat, Mother Julie would sometimes take over the household chores, including the cooking. In her free time, she also liked to work in the garden.

In Namur Mother Julie personally supervised the remodeling of a large house into a convent. At the same time she tended to the basic needs of the sisters. She helped with the washing and the shopping. The community was so poor that the sisters didn't have enough cloaks to wear to church. They had to go to Mass in different shifts. But Mother Julie managed to make sure that they always had enough to eat.

She also took care to nourish their spiritual lives.

Julie urged her sisters to value prayer. She said, "Without prayer there is no Sister of Notre Dame." She taught them to focus on God saying, "Our hearts should be simpler than crystal, for crystal reflects all the colors of the rainbow, while the heart of a Sister of Notre Dame should reflect nothing but God alone."

Mother Julie was always a realist. She warned the sisters that the challenging times they lived in meant that they would not see many results from their work. She encouraged them by saying, "We must be satisfied with doing our duty well and trying to give good example. Then leave everything to the mercy of the good God. That is what the good God asks of us."

At the same time, Julie taught her sisters and prepared them to be teachers. She and they gave themselves to serving the poor, which Julie saw as the main work of her congregation. She loved to remind her sisters, "We exist only for the poor, absolutely only for the poor."

The sisters' work made many demands on them. For Mother Julie, in a special way, it involved much travel.

16

JOURNEYS

In twelve years, Julie made one hundred and twenty journeys. She opened new convents and closed others. She visited the sisters and even returned to Amiens several times. Travel in those days wasn't easy, especially for a woman her age. There was danger from robbers, floods, mud and even winds strong enough to blow people over. Julie often had to go on foot. People called her the "walking love of God." One innkeeper invited her to dine free of charge at his best table whenever she stopped at his place. He explained, "Mother Julie's conversation and humor brighten my inn."

One day Julie could find no transportation back to Namur other than a horse. A boy was to go with her to bring the horse back. He ran alongside with a whip in case the horse needed encouraging.

"Here's a pond. The horse can have a drink and we can rest a bit," Julie suggested to the boy at one point. They stopped and she dismounted.

After a brief rest, they were ready to travel again. Mother Julie climbed back into the saddle. Without thinking, the boy cracked the whip. The startled horse backed into the deep pond.

"Oh!" cried the shocked boy, "Whoa! Whoa!"

The water was almost to Julie's waist. She gripped the saddle tightly, trying to keep her balance. "Guardian Angel," she prayed, "help me!"

Just then the horse lunged forward toward the bank of the pond. Mother Julie was safe but half-soaked. Afterwards she enjoyed telling the story.

Julie had another even more terrifying experience. Once she was riding in a carriage with five or six men. One of them, a very large man, was drunk. At midnight this man leaned out of the coach. "Stop!" he shouted to the driver. But the driver didn't hear. Thinking the driver's whip was meant for him, the drunken man attacked the coachman. Pulling him to the ground, he began to beat him. Mother Julie and her fellow travelers were now in a runaway carriage! The drunken man ran after them and eventually caught up to the carriage. He ran alongside it.

"What did you do with the driver?" one of the passengers shouted.

"I threw him in a ditch," the attacker replied.

Hearing this, the remaining men leaped from the coach to try to help the wounded driver. And the drunken man climbed in with Mother Julie! The horses ran wildly until they finally decided to stop. One of the passengers who had jumped out then ran up and did his best to steer the horses to the next town, where the drunken man was arrested. Two days later the beaten driver died.

Another time Julie walked thirty-seven miles back to Namur carrying her travel bag. She also carried her cloak rolled up under her arm, for it was hot. At one point two soldiers from Napoleon's army joined her on the dusty road. Mother Julie was glad for their company. It made her feel safer. The soldiers matched their steps to hers every once in a while. As they talked about battles, one loyal officer boasted, "I would give my last drop of blood for Emperor Napoleon."

And I, thought Julie, *shouldn't I give my all to my God and the spread of his Kingdom?*

Mother Julie also had to make some unpleasant journeys in order to recover a large sum of money that Father de Sambucy had borrowed from her community. He even pleaded with Julie to reunite her former convent in Amiens (now occupied by the sisters under Bishop Demandolx's direction) with her convent in Namur—just so he wouldn't have to give up the money. Julie answered, "When a king exiles someone, the king must bring him back." She meant that Bishop Demandolx had sent her away from Amiens, and only he could call her back.

In the end Mother Julie was given the money in the form of two baskets of silver coins. These were so heavy that she could barely move them. Many people helped her on her trip back to Belgium. At an inn she had put some eggs on top of one of the baskets of coins. When a carriage driver lifted the baskets, he observed, "Well, little lady, you've got some mighty heavy eggs in here. I'd like to have some of those myself." This frightened Julie, but she managed to get the money safely to Belgium without being robbed.

Two years later Father de Sambucy, who had gotten involved in politics, was imprisoned. Other priests in Amiens who wanted Mother Julie to return wrote letters begging her to come back.

They brought their idea to Bishop Demandolx.

17

BACK TO AMIENS

Mother Julie couldn't believe her eyes. She read the letter she held again. It was from Bishop Demandolx. "I wish to see you back in Amiens," he wrote. "I want you to resume the office of superior of the Sisters of Notre Dame in my diocese. I dismissed you through an error of judgment on my part, because I relied on a person whom I thought I could trust."

But a merchant who had just returned to Namur from Amiens warned Julie, "Your former convent is in debt. Be careful about taking responsibility for it."

After a long period of reflection, prayer, and consultation with the other sisters, Mother Julie said to Sister Catherine, "Come with me to Amiens. Let's find out what God wishes for us there."

The trip was treacherous. The carriage almost overturned several times. The two sisters arrived at Amiens in the middle of the night. They had to go to three inns before they found one where they could stay.

Totally exhausted, they fell on the bed without sheets.

The next day Sister Marie, the superior at Amiens who was on loan from another religious community, came for Mother Julie and Sister Catherine. As they approached Mother Julie's former convent, Julie had a vision. She saw Jesus carrying his cross away from the convent. He looked at her, and in her heart Julie heard the words, "Look at me and follow me."

Mother Julie went straight to work. She found a larger house for the fourteen sisters at Amiens. They were told they could live there rent-free in return for teaching girls who worked at a local factory. Julie intended to use the sale of the original house to pay off the sisters' debts. Everything seemed to be working out well, and Mother Julie returned to Namur. No sooner had she gotten home than the plans fell apart. She received a letter from Sister Marie.

"Look at this!" Mother Julie exclaimed to the sisters. "Sister Marie writes that the new housing for the sisters in Amiens is not to be free after all. Besides that, the man who had intended to purchase our old house has changed his mind. But that's not all. Sister

Marie also says it's time for her to return to her own community."

"I think God is telling us something," one sister quietly said.

"Yes," sighed Mother Julie, recalling her vision of Jesus leaving. "We must close the house at Amiens."

Bishop Demandolx agreed with Julie. The house was closed, and the sisters went to other convents or home to their families. Eventually Mother Victoire, who had caused Mother Julie so much grief, left religious life.

Once Amiens was settled, Mother Julie concentrated on her other houses. She visited the sisters and saw that the children were learning. At one poor school the principal had turned the courtyard into a potato garden. "Where can the children play now?" Mother Julie asked. "Where can the sisters walk in the fresh air and sunshine? Call the children out for an extra recess. Have them jump and dance on these plants and put the round stones back in the courtyard. Trust God to provide food for you."

Later that year as the sisters strolled around the courtyard, one cried out, "Look at the leaves between the stones." She stooped and tugged at the stems, and several potatoes popped out of the soil. When all the stones were lifted up, enough potatoes were unearthed to feed the sisters and children for the entire winter!

18

VISIT TO THE POPE

Pope Pius VII, along with the Church in France, was being persecuted by Napoleon. After three years of house arrest in one town, the Pope was forced to travel to a palace in Fountainebleau (FOHN tehn BLOW), a town outside of Paris. Pope Pius was already very sick, and the journey under the blazing sun almost killed him. In 1813 Mother Julie decided to visit him. She wanted to ask his blessing on all her sisters and to pledge her loyalty to him. Father LeBlanc arranged an audience for her.

"Come, Madeleine," Mother Julie invited a novice. "I'd like you to go with me to Fountainebleau."

The two women took turns riding a borrowed donkey for forty-five miles. When they reached the palace, Mother Julie instructed the younger sister, "Stay here in the courtyard and take care of the donkey."

After quite a while, Julie emerged from the palace, her face red and swollen from crying.

"Mother Julie!" Madeleine exclaimed. "Are you all right?"

"My daughter," Julie replied, "I have seen the Holy Father. We have wept together over the troubles of the Church."

Mother Julie held out a crucifix. "See. He has given me this as a gift."

All the way home Julie held the crucifix and could hardly talk.

In time all the convents in France had to be closed, and the Sisters of Notre Dame lived and worked only in Belgium. Mother Julie wrote to Sister Françoise, "What a large heart one must have to be a Sister of Notre Dame! What strong medicine one must be able to swallow! This is the grace I ask for all my daughters—that they may be very courageous, very generous."

Mother Julie kept in touch with all her sisters. In the evening she wrote letters by the glow of a candle. Today these letters fill seven volumes of books. They reveal her love for the sisters. She was concerned about everyone and everything. At Christmas she wrote, "My love to you all, and I hug you all like pincers!" (Pincers are a tool used for gripping things.) Sometimes Julie advised a sister, "Try to practice your spelling a little," or "Eat wisely to do the work of the good God." To one she wrote, "I am sending you a basket of peas and carrots." She asked another, "Have you had a pig bought?" To many sisters she wrote, "Courage, my dear good daughter."

Courage was greatly needed as Napoleon's empire crumbled and troops invaded the cities. Soon enough the dangerous situation brought a halt to Mother Julie's trips and letter writing.

19

WAR

In 1813 the Allies, countries that had joined forces against Napoleon's empire, extended him a peace offer. Napoleon hesitated in accepting it, so the Allies took it back. Foreign soldiers swarmed into the cities, including Namur. The soldiers, looking for places to stay, took over houses. They helped themselves to supplies and attacked the women. Food was scarce. It was very difficult for Mother Julie to feed the seventy sisters and children under her care.

One day Julie sent a sister down to the cellar to bring up some vegetables.

The sister returned shortly. "Mother Julie," she said. "I'm sorry, but there's nothing left."

"Go back again, my daughter," directed Julie. "The good God will make you find what we need."

This time the sister came back carrying food for the next meal!

Mother Julie hid the community's valuables. A front door reinforced with thirteen

This time the sister came back with food!

boards and a strong bar kept the sisters from harm. So did numerous prayers. Sometimes Julie prayed through the night. From chapel she could hear the soldiers pounding on the door. She entrusted her sisters, the children, and herself to God's provident care.

As soon as Napoleon formally gave up his power and there was peace, Mother Julie set out to visit her sisters again. She even opened a new convent.

But in 1815 Napoleon rallied and his army attacked. Now the war came to Belgium. The sisters could see the fighting from their windows.

After Napoleon's defeat at the Battle of Waterloo, thousands of soldiers roamed the streets. More than once a group of these hungry men broke into a convent and terrified the sisters. Providentially no one was hurt, although some convents were ransacked and damaged. One young Sister of Notre Dame, however, never recovered from the shocking experience and died soon after it.

The city of Namur was spared destruction. The Prussian general at the city gates had heard how kind the people had been to the soldiers. "Stop firing the cannon!" he ordered, "There's no resistance anyway." The French had run out of ammunition.

By the time the war ended, Mother Julie was worn out with worry and stress. She became ill. But God had still another cross for her, and she expected it. Julie remembered Father Enfantin foretelling her crosses many years before. She confided to Sister Françoise, "Daughter, there is still one more trial I must endure."

"No, Mother," responded Françoise. "That can't be. You went through enough at Amiens!"

"It was predicted that I should be persecuted by bishops, priests, *and* the sisters," Mother Julie explained. "All is not over yet."

And it wasn't.

The worst was yet to come.

20

SUSPICION

When Napoleon took over Church affairs he even had the catechism rewritten. He removed from office any of the bishops who protested. But he left Bishop Pisani, the bishop of Namur, alone. Bishop Pisani had been appointed by Napoleon before being approved by Rome. Napoleon would not change one of his own appointments. Besides, one of Napoleon's ministers was also a friend of the bishop's. Some people became suspicious of Bishop Pisani and doubted his loyalty to the Church.

"I wonder why Bishop Pisani is still head of our diocese while other bishops have been removed," mused a sister one day.

"Well," whispered her companion, "I've heard he's one of Napoleon's men. He's betrayed his Church for his emperor."

"It's a wonder then that Mother Julie supports Bishop Pisani," shot back the first sister.

"Maybe she's secretly working against the Church too!" came the answer.

These fears were unfounded. Mother Julie was always loyal to the Church. But because she treated Bishop Pisani with obedience and respect, some of her sisters began to doubt her loyalty to the Pope and to the Church. They complained about her to their bishops.

Julie also came under fire from her own sisters regarding their rule of life. Some young sisters thought that the proposed rule should be kept very strictly, with no exceptions ever made for special needs or emergencies. Mother Julie made changes in it when she thought it was necessary. After all, it was not yet the final rule approved by the Church.

The critical sisters complained, "We're all supposed to do the same things at the same time every day. But Mother Julie wants us to work our activities around the needs of people."

Mother Julie remarked to Sister Françoise, "I do not adhere slavishly to a regulation when I see a greater good to be done, because for us nothing is really settled yet." More than once when Mother Julie met with unexplainable trials, she reminded Françoise and herself, "It's God's work, not ours."

The pain Julie's own sisters caused her was excruciating and made her cry many tears. Some of the sisters who doubted her and criticized her had been with her from the early days of the community.

Julie began to think that maybe she was at fault. When Bishop Pisani heard that, he confided to Sister Françoise, "The only fault I can accuse her of is that she's killing herself by not taking care of her health."

He was right.

21

WITH THE GOOD GOD

In December of 1815, Mother Julie slipped on steps that were being washed and fell backwards. She fainted, and two sisters carried her to her room. Despite a terrible headache, Julie went back to work.

By the middle of January, though, Mother Julie was so ill that she couldn't leave Namur. For three months she alternated between periods of terrific pain and some good days. She lost her appetite and couldn't stand even the slightest noise. Everyone was praying for a cure, but it was not to be.

Mother Julie's last days echoed her whole life. She suffered much pain, but never lost confidence in God. When she heard that a child from one of their schools was upset about her illness, Mother Julie sent for her. "My little Thérèse," she said gently, "don't be sad. God has no more use for me here. He is calling me home to himself now." The girl sobbed and buried her head in Julie's quilt. "Have courage, child,"

Mother Julie soothed. "You are the friend of the good God, and he is so good."

Sister Françoise spent hours with Mother Julie. She read to her as she had in the old days when Julie was an invalid. One day Julie said, "Françoise, my dear friend, I beg your forgiveness for any way that I have hurt you."

Trying to hold back her tears and squeezing Julie's hand, Françoise replied, "I forgive you. But honestly, I can only remember love and goodness from you."

Sorrow and fatigue took their toll on Sister Françoise. She too became seriously ill. Both she and Mother Julie received Viaticum on the same day.

Sisters took turns watching by Mother Julie's bed. Suddenly they heard her singing the "Magnificat," her favorite hymn. This song of Mary's praise and joy begins with the words, "My soul magnifies the Lord, and my spirit rejoices in God my savior." When Mother Julie finished the hymn, she became unconscious. She died very peacefully with a smile on her lips at two o'clock the next morning. It was April 8, 1816. Julie had gone to meet her good God face to face.

Word spread quickly through the city, "The saint is dead! The saint is dead!" It wasn't until 1906 that the Church beatified Mother Julie and gave her the title "Blessed" in a ceremony in Rome. Finally, on June 22, 1969 Mother Julie Billiart was officially canonized or proclaimed a saint by the Catholic Church.

After Julie's death, Françoise slowly recovered. She became the new superior general. Under her guidance Mother Julie's congregation, the Sisters of Notre Dame of Namur, flourished and spread. In time, two other separate congregations were established from the Sisters of Notre Dame founded by Mother Julie. One was located in Amersfoort, Holland and the other in Coesfeld, Germany. Today Sisters of Notre Dame from all three congregations continue Saint Julie's work and live according to her spirit. All over the world and in many different ways they echo her message, "How good is the good God!"

PRAYER

Saint Julie, just as the sunflower keeps its face turned toward the sun, you always kept your heart and mind turned toward God. You showed your deep love for God in prayer and action. Even in great sufferings and trials you used to repeat, "How good God is!" And you meant it.

Ask God to give me strong faith, Saint Julie. Help me to see his goodness in my life. I want to be like you. I want to spread the news of God's goodness and love for us whenever and however I can. I look forward to meeting you in heaven, where we'll enjoy this love and God's presence forever! Pray for me, Saint Julie. Amen.

GLOSSARY

1. **Angelus** — a prayer honoring Jesus' Incarnation, that mystery in which the Second Person of the Trinity became a human being through the cooperation of Mary. The Angelus consists of three verses, each concluding with a Hail Mary. It is traditionally prayed three times a day: at 6:00 AM, at noon, and at 6:00 PM.

2. **Beatification** — a step toward the Church's declaring someone a saint. In the ceremony of beatification the person who is beatified is given the title Blessed and may be honored as such.

3. **Blasphemy** — irreverent and abusive language toward God, the Church, or the saints.

4. **Canonization** — the ceremony in which the Church officially declares someone a saint, a person who is in heaven. To canonize someone is to recognize that he or she has lived a life of heroic virtue, is worthy of imitation and can intercede for others.

5. **Chastity** — the virtue which consists in using the gift of sexuality as God intended for one's state of life. For religious, this means remaining unmarried.

6. **Confessor** — (as used in this book) a priest who is authorized to hear confessions and celebrate the sacrament of Reconciliation with a person.

7. **Confraternity** — an association whose members undertake certain prayers and/or apostolic works.

8. **Contemplation** — a deep form of prayer in which a person is completely absorbed in the presence of God.

9. **Diocese** — a territory made up of parishes placed by the Pope under the care of a Church leader called a bishop.

10. **First Friday** — the first Friday of the month; people receive Communion on nine consecutive first Fridays to show devotion to the Sacred Heart of Jesus.

11. **Founder** — the person who begins a religious congregation and gives it its special spirit and work.

12. **Monastery** — the dwelling place of communities of men or women religious who live in seclusion.

13. **Novena** — praying a special prayer for nine consecutive days or on the same day of nine consecutive weeks. The custom is based on the nine days when Mary and the apostles waited and prayed in the Upper Room for the coming of the Holy Spirit on Pentecost.

14. **Oath** — the solemn invoking of the name of God to witness to the truth of one's words.

15. **Pilgrimage** — a journey made to a holy place or shrine in order to pray and feel closer to God.

16. **Retreat** — a period of withdrawing from the world and everyday activities to spend time in prayer, reflection, and other spiritual activities.

17. **Revolution** — a great social, cultural, and political upheaval begun in order to bring about a change.

18. **Rule** — (as used in this book) the laws that members of a religious congregation follow in living their unique lifestyle in the spirit of their founder. The rule is approved by the Church.

19. **Viaticum** — the reception of Holy Communion by someone who is dying.

Jesus comes to the person to help him or her make the journey to eternal life.

20. **Vow** — a solemn promise freely made to God. Members of religious communities usually make vows of poverty, chastity, and obedience.

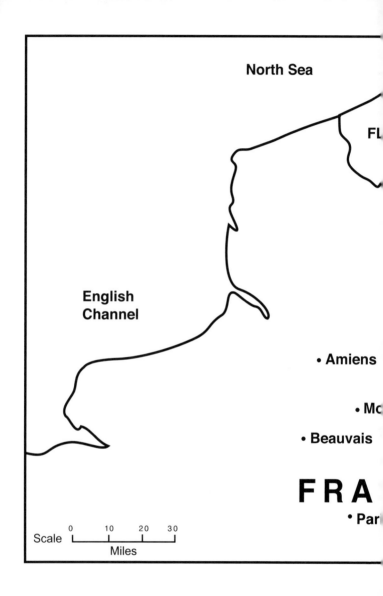

North Sea

FL

English
Channel

• Amiens

• Mo

• Beauvais

F R A

• Par

Scale 0   10   20   30
       Miles

RS

• Ghent   • St. Nicholas

BELGIUM

• Jumet   • Namur

er

Illy

mpiègne

E

Daughters of St. Paul

I We Pray I We Preach I We Praise I

Centering our lives on Jesus, Way, Truth & Life

Witnessing to the joy of living totally for Jesus

Sharing Jesus with people through various forms of media: books, music, video, & multimedia

If you would like more information on following Jesus and spreading His Gospel

as a Daughter of St. Paul...

contact:

Vocation Director
Daughters of St. Paul
50 Saint Pauls Avenue
Boston, MA 02130-3491
(617) 522-8911
e-mail: vocations@pauline.org
or visit www.pauline.org

Pauline
BOOKS & MEDIA

The Daughters of St. Paul operate book and media centers at the following addresses. Visit, call or write the one nearest you today, or find us on the World Wide Web, www.pauline.org

California
3908 Sepulveda Blvd, Culver City,
  CA 90230   310-397-8676
5945 Balboa Avenue, San Diego,
  CA 92111   858-565-9181
46 Geary Street, San Francisco,
  CA 94108   415-781-5180

Florida
145 S.W. 107th Avenue, Miami,
  FL 33174   305-559-6715

Hawaii
1143 Bishop Street, Honolulu, HI
  96813   808-521-2731

Neighbor Islands call: 800-259-8463

Illinois
172 North Michigan Avenue, Chicago,
  IL 60601   312-346-4228

Louisiana
4403 Veterans Memorial Blvd,
  Metairie, LA 70006   504-887-7631

Massachusetts
Rte. 1, 885 Providence Hwy,
  Dedham, MA 02026
  781-326-5385

Missouri
9804 Watson Road, St. Louis,
  MO 63126   314-965-3512

New Jersey
561 U.S. Route 1, Wick Plaza,
  Edison, NJ 08817
  732-572-1200

New York
150 East 52nd Street,
  New York, NY 10022
  212-754-1110
78 Fort Place, Staten Island, NY
  10301   718-447-5071

Ohio
2105 Ontario Street, Cleveland,
  OH 44115   216-621-9427

Pennsylvania
9171-A Roosevelt Blvd,
  Philadelphia, PA 19114
  215-676-9494

South Carolina
243 King Street, Charleston, SC
  29401   843-577-0175

Tennessee
4811 Poplar Avenue, Memphis,
  TN 38117   901-761-2987

Texas
114 Main Plaza, San Antonio, TX
  78205   210-224-8101

Virginia
1025 King Street, Alexandria, VA
  22314   703-549-3806

Canada
3022 Dufferin Street, Toronto,
  Ontario, Canada M6B 3T5
  416-781-9131
1155 Yonge Street, Toronto, Ontario,
  Canada M4T 1W2   416-934-3440

¡También somos su fuente para libros, videos y música en español!